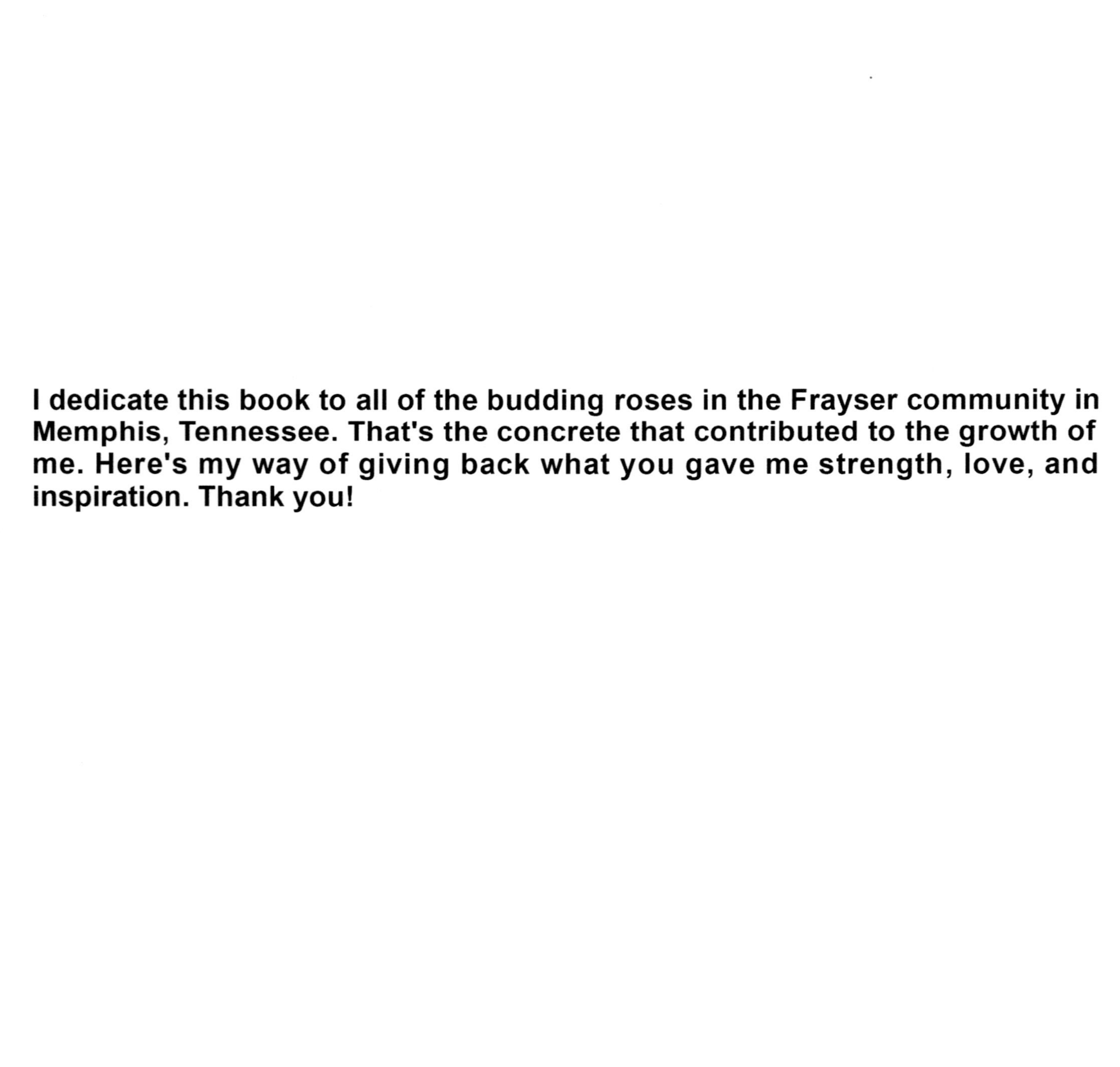

I dedicate this book to all of the budding roses in the Frayser community in Memphis, Tennessee. That's the concrete that contributed to the growth of me. Here's my way of giving back what you gave me strength, love, and inspiration. Thank you!

STILL A ROSE

By T'Arrah Marjé
ILLUSTRATED BY CAMERON WILSON

SNACKS

A rose is still a rose no matter where it grows. I see one growing through the concrete. I am like the rose and the rose is like me.

Don't ask me why this rose still grows toward the sun and the sky despite its circumstances. A better question is how does it continue to grow, stand tall, and take its chances.

Maybe it is because this rose knows it serves a greater purpose. Maybe despite its situation it knows it is worth it. I am like the rose and the rose is like me.

No, every flower is not the same, but the facts about each one that grows still remain. The soil is rich, and I promise you this...The sun shines on it just the same.

Its petals are just as red. Its roots are just as strong. They may be even stronger, because to break through pavement, it must have a lot of armor.

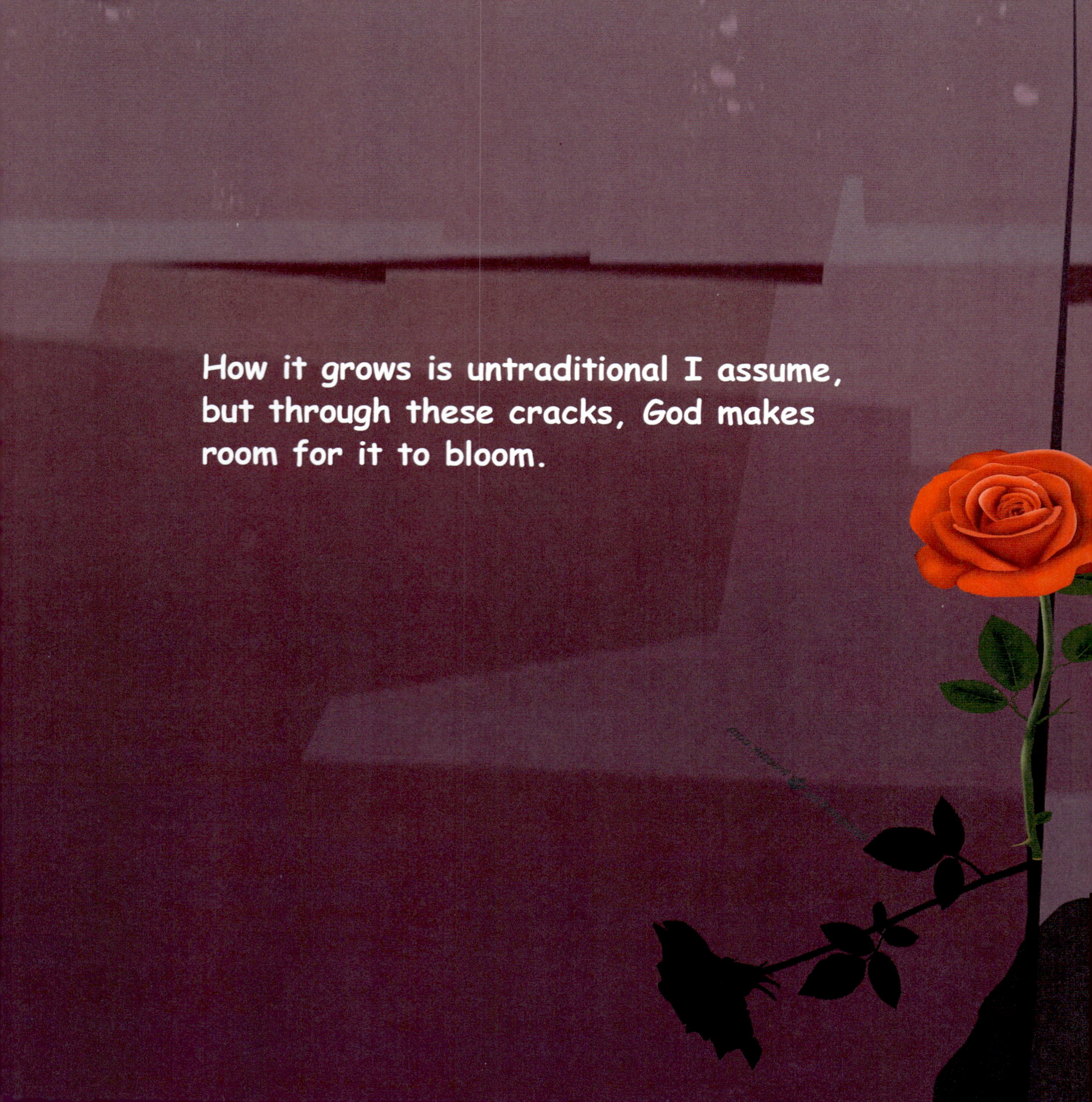

How it grows is untraditional I assume, but through these cracks, God makes room for it to bloom.

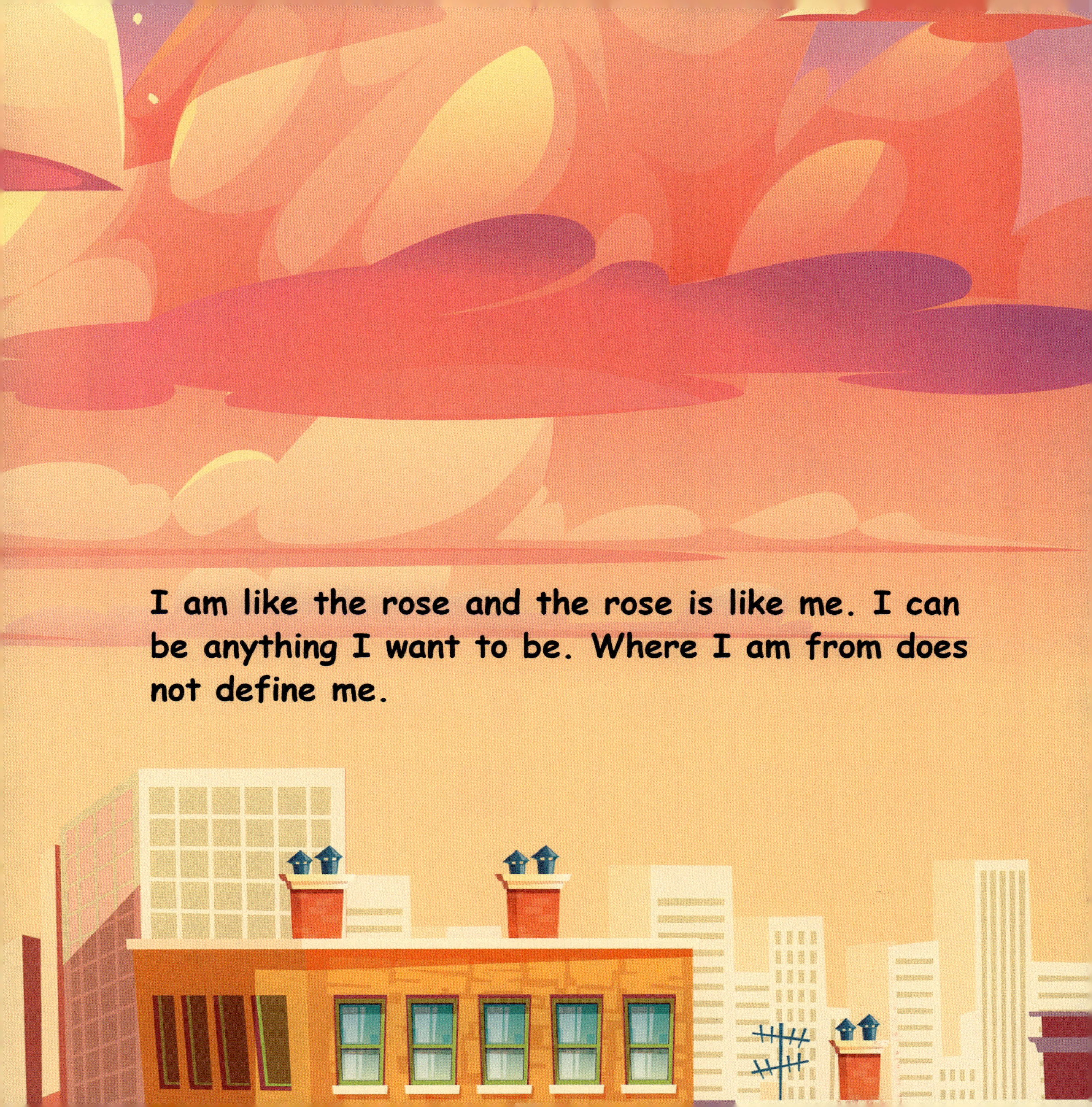

I am like the rose and the rose is like me. I can be anything I want to be. Where I am from does not define me.

I do not have to be what I see around me every day. I have my own mind. That means I can make my own way.

GROCERY STORE

I am marching to the beat of my own drum. It does not matter who I am around or where I am from. I define me not the world. This is true for every boy and girl. Who cares if I'm different? I will not let it stop me from being prolific.

A rose is still a rose no matter where it grows. Whether it grows from a bush, concrete, or a flower pot, the point is to never be confused about who you are or what you got.

Wherever your roots are planted, there is still potential to be whoever you want to be on this planet, because a rose is still a rose no matter where it grows.

STILL A

Whenever anyone sees a rose they cannot feel anything but happiness inside.

Be proud of who you are and where you are from. Do not shy away from having your moment in the sun. As a flower you need the light, and the light needs you. So bloom big and strong to show the world what is true. A rose is still a rose no matter where it grows.

Made in the USA
Middletown, DE
20 January 2021

32122597R00015